BOLIVIA

...in Pictures

Courtesy of United Nations

Visual Geography Series®

BOLIVIA

...in Pictures

Prepared by
Geography Department

Lerner Publications Company
Minneapolis

Independent Picture Service

**These Indian children live near La Paz, where it is cool
enough to wear wool caps and heavy pullovers.**

This book is an all-new edition in the Visual Geography Series. Previous editions were published by
Sterling Publishing Company, New York City. The
text, set in 10/12 Century Textbook, is fully revised
and updated, and new photographs, maps, charts, and
captions have been added.

LIBRARY OF CONGRESS CATALOGING-IN-PUBLICATION DATA

Bolivia in pictures.

(Visual geography series)
Rev. ed. of: Bolivia in pictures.
Includes index.
Summary: An introduction to the geography, history,
government, people, and economy of the landlocked
country of Bolivia.
1. Bolivia. [1. Bolivia] I. Bailey, Bernadine, 1901– .
Bolivia in pictures. II. Lerner Publications Company.
Geography Dept. III. Series: Visual geography series
(Minneapolis, Minn.)
F3308.B688   1987   984   86–33821
ISBN 0-8225-1808-2 (lib. bdg.)

International Standard Book Number: 0-8225-1808-2
Library of Congress Catalog Card Number: 86-33821

VISUAL GEOGRAPHY SERIES®

Publisher
Harry Jonas Lerner
Associate Publisher
Nancy M. Campbell
Executive Series Editor
Mary M. Rodgers
Assistant Series Editor
Gretchen Bratvold
Editorial Assistant
Nora W. Kniskern
Illustrations Editors
Nathan A. Haverstock
Karen A. Sirvaitis
Consultants/Contributors
Dr. Ruth F. Hale
Nathan A. Haverstock
Sandra K. Davis
Designer
Jim Simondet
Cartographer
Carol F. Barrett
Indexer
Kristine S. Schubert
Production Manager
Gary J. Hansen

Independent Picture Service

**Indian homes on the shores of Lake Titicaca have thatched
roofs and walls of stone and adobe.**

Acknowledgments

Title page photo courtesy of Inter-American Development Bank.

Elevation contours adapted from *The Times Atlas of
the World*, seventh comprehensive edition (New York:
Times Books, 1985).

4 5 6 7 8 9 10 96 95 94 93

Courtesy of United Nations

Visible from all parts of the capital city of La Paz, snow-covered Mount Illimani rises 21,201 feet above sea level.

Contents

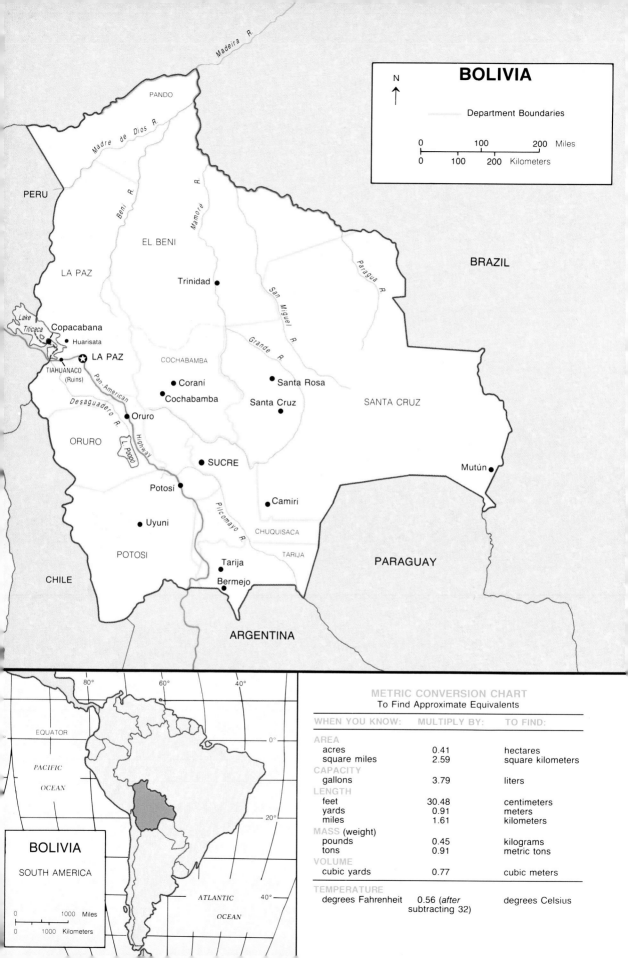

BOLIVIA

N

Department Boundaries

| 0 | 100 | 200 | Miles |
| 0 | 100 | 200 | Kilometers |

PANDO

Madeira R.

Madre de Dios R.

PERU

Beni R.

Mamoré R.

EL BENI

LA PAZ

Trinidad

Paraguá R.

BRAZIL

Lake Titicaca

Copacabana

Huarisata

San Miguel R.

LA PAZ

TIAHUANACO (Ruins)

COCHABAMBA

Corani

Cochabamba

Grande R.

Santa Rosa

Santa Cruz

SANTA CRUZ

Desaguadero R.

Pan American

Oruro

ORURO

L. Poopó

Highway

SUCRE

Mutún

Potosí

Camiri

Uyuni

Pilcomayo R.

CHUQUISACA

POTOSI

TARIJA

PARAGUAY

Tarija

Bermejo

CHILE

ARGENTINA

BOLIVIA

SOUTH AMERICA

| 0 | 1000 | Miles |
| 0 | 1000 | Kilometers |

80° 60° 40°

EQUATOR 0°

PACIFIC OCEAN

20°

40°

ATLANTIC OCEAN

METRIC CONVERSION CHART
To Find Approximate Equivalents

WHEN YOU KNOW:	MULTIPLY BY:	TO FIND:
AREA		
acres	0.41	hectares
square miles	2.59	square kilometers
CAPACITY		
gallons	3.79	liters
LENGTH		
feet	30.48	centimeters
yards	0.91	meters
miles	1.61	kilometers
MASS (weight)		
pounds	0.45	kilograms
tons	0.91	metric tons
VOLUME		
cubic yards	0.77	cubic meters
TEMPERATURE		
degrees Fahrenheit	0.56 (*after* subtracting 32)	degrees Celsius

At a market in La Paz, Bolivians of all classes and backgrounds meet to do business.

Introduction

Bolivia, a poor country in South America, is a land of contrasts, with towering snowcapped mountains and moist, hot jungles. On the streets of its Andean cities—the highest settlements in the Americas—university-trained mining engineers coexist with Indians who live and dress much as they did before the arrival of their Spanish conquerors.

Once, the country's dependence upon a few mineral exports made it exceptionally vulnerable to outside forces. Leaders were more intent on promoting their own interests than those of the nation. Since achieving independence, Bolivia has lost more than half of its national territory to its more powerful neighbors, Chile, Brazil, and Paraguay—including the land that provided Bolivia with its own access to the Pacific Ocean.

For more than a thousand years, the territory of present-day Bolivia was a far-off province of the Inca Empire. For three centuries after its conquest, the future nation of Bolivia was exploited by Spain. Spanish monarchs were more interested in the production of Bolivia's mines than in the welfare of its people.

Bolivia was scarcely even a unified region when it achieved nationhood. Indeed, its very independence was won for it by outsiders, who fought under the banner of

7

South America's Venezuelan-born liberator, Simon Bolívar. With independence thrust upon it, Bolivia faced the still-unfinished task of forging a national identity amid cultural and geographical diversity.

The diversity extends to the very physical nature of the people. In the elevated places where most Bolivians live, people have developed larger lungs to take in enough oxygen in the thin atmosphere. During preconquest times the Incas had two armies to compensate for the thin air —one for the highlands, the other for the lowlands.

To further complicate Bolivia's task of creating a single nation from a diverse people, the country's Indians, who constitute the majority today, were treated with extraordinary cruelty by their Spanish conquerors. Once the Spaniards learned that Bolivia possessed the richest silver mine in the New World, they forced the Indians to dig out the precious metal from veins deep in the earth. Diseases common to miners but complicated by cold weather and high elevation cut short the lives of the Indians. The same harsh conditions prevailed on farms, where Indians were forced into servitude to cultivate the fields

Independent Picture Service

This statue of Simon Bolívar, who liberated Bolivia from Spanish rule, stands prominently on Sixteenth of July Avenue in La Paz.

for masters whose descendants today comprise Bolivia's landowning aristocracy.

Even today only the most fortunate or progressive of the Indian majority speak the official Spanish language of the middle and upper classes. In times of economic

Independent Picture Service

At San José mine in the town of Oruro, small train cars carry away tin ore to be processed into a more-refined metal.

On the border of Bolivia and Peru at an elevation of 12,500 feet, Lake Titicaca provides fish for local consumption as well as many attractions for visitors. The ruins of Tiahuanaco and some Incan remains are nearby.

growth, present-day Bolivians seek the comforts of other consumer societies through the evolution of their economy and the exploitation of minerals and energy resources. Some Bolivians have turned to the illegal drug trade, which has become the country's most important moneymaker. Cocaine-producing laboratories in Bolivia are primary targets of U.S. and Bolivian officials, who are waging a war against drug cartels. Bolivian authorities have cooperated with U.S. troops to destroy undercover factories that process cocaine for the U.S. market.

In this century, Bolivia has experienced a revolution whose goal was the creation of a framework for lasting social justice. The revolution, which exploded in 1952, has yet to run its course. After suffering from an inflation rate that reached 24,000 percent in the mid-1980s, Bolivia's economy is slowly recovering. Although unemployment and wide gaps between classes still exist, Bolivia is addressing its economic and political problems. In the early 1990s, conditions in the country, once considered the poorest in South America, had improved.

Women harvest coca leaves near Coroico. The Indians chew the leaves to ease hunger pains. Much of Bolivia's coca production, however, is processed into the drug cocaine and shipped to foreign markets such as the United States.

Sheep and alpacas are raised for their wool in the Bolivian Highlands.

1) The Land

Deep in the heart of the South American continent lies the landlocked Republic of Bolivia. With an area of 424,162 square miles, Bolivia is roughly twice as large as the state of Texas.

Though still a sizable country, Bolivia since gaining independence has lost more than half of its national territory through both wars and treaties. The nation's neighbors—which have figured into these ter-

ritorial losses—are Peru to the northwest, Chile to the southwest, Argentina to the south, Paraguay to the southeast, and Brazil to the east and the north.

Western Bolivia, where most Bolivians live, is a mountainous and mineral-rich area. Eastern Bolivia, though mountainous in some areas, is much lower and more level. Farmers there raise a wide variety of crops—especially along the eastern border, where the hills give way to gently rolling tropical lowlands and forests.

Topography

HIGHLANDS

Three great chains, or cordilleras, of the Andes cut across Bolivia, extending 500 miles from the northwest to the southeast and towering to heights of over 20,000 feet. The range farthest west is the Cordillera Occidental, or western chain, the middle range is the Cordillera Real, or royal chain, and the eastern range is the Cordillera Oriental, or eastern chain.

Between these mountain ranges are 12,000-foot-high plateaus, collectively called the altiplano. The only other place in the world where people live on land as high as this is Tibet, in central Asia. Living at high altitudes is not easy because of the cold weather and the lack of oxygen in the air. Snow-topped mountains rise skyward for thousands of feet from their bases on the altiplano. Four mountain peaks in western Bolivia rank among the highest in the world. Bolivia's highest peak is Ancohuma at 21,489 feet, followed by Sajama at 21,391 feet, and Illimani at 21,201 feet. On the Chilean border is Mount Tocorpuri at 19,137 feet.

To the east of the towering Cordillera Oriental are semitropical valleys—called yungas, the Aymara Indian term for hills —which range in altitude from 2,000 to 6,500 feet. The yungas are extremely scenic, with steep, mountain hillsides, deep, narrow gorges, and lush, subtropical forests. Several popular health resorts in the yungas are frequented by Bolivians in search of natural beauty not found in the often-barren settings of higher elevations. The fertile yungas have long produced much of Bolivia's food, and their forests provide many commercially valuable trees.

The two most important crops of this region are coffee beans of exceptional quality and coca leaves, from which cocaine is produced. Since Incan times Indians have practiced the custom of chewing

Photo by José Armando Araneda

Among the highest mountains in the world, the Andes dominate nearly two-fifths of Bolivia. For centuries Indians have resided in the area and have adapted to living at high altitudes.

Although an all-weather road connects La Paz and the yungas, the steep, winding route is difficult and rises over 11,250 feet in about 50 miles.

coca leaves to gain energy and to conquer hunger.

LOWLANDS

Recent years have seen a dramatic expansion of both farming and cattle raising in Bolivia's lowland plain, or llano. The lowlands are watered by rivers that rise in the Andes and traverse rolling and level terrain. Some of these rivers, fed by the melting snow high up in the Andes, flow northward and eventually reach the Madeira River of Brazil, which, in turn, empties into the mighty Amazon. The Beni, Mamoré, Grande, San Miguel, and Paragua rivers are just a few of the rivers that feed into Brazil's Madeira River.

Smaller rivers, such as the Pilcomayo, drain southeastern Bolivia before finding their way into the huge River Plate Basin, which, with its tributaries, drains about two-thirds of southern South America.

To spur the development of the lowlands, the Bolivian government, with financial assistance from international agencies, has undertaken extensive programs to attract new settlers from land-poor regions of the country. Unfortunately, the production of marijuana, the growing of coca, and the processing of cocaine for foreign markets have also boosted the economy in some lowland areas.

In the southeast, the lowlands of Bolivia merge with the Chaco region of neighbor-

Independent Picture Service

Government officials inspect earth-moving equipment at a resettlement site in the lowlands. For several years the Bolivian government has encouraged people from the poor lands of the altiplano to relocate in the rich, but underdeveloped, lands of the Amazon region.

ing Paraguay. This is an area of scattered forests and poor soil—conditions found on both sides of the border.

Climate

Although Bolivia is located within the tropics, most Bolivians live at altitudes where the climate is much colder than might be expected. In the altiplano the air is clear, and it is generally cool and dry. The temperature averages 55° F in January and only 40° F in July.

In contrast, the climate in the yungas is warm and humid. Temperatures there and in the lower valleys of south central Bolivia average 72° F in January and 52° F in July. Most of the northern and eastern lowlands are also warm and humid with average daily temperatures of 75° F all year round.

In most regions of Bolivia the summer (December through February) is a rainy season. Droughts occur frequently in the highlands, though summer mornings are often rainy and cold. In the lowlands rain-

Courtesy of Inter-American Development Bank

About 40 percent of Bolivia's population lives on the altiplano between two lofty ranges of the Andes. Many of these people reside in small communities where life has changed little over the centuries.

Photo by José Armando Araneda

Indians make *balsas de tortora,* or boats of reed, for fishing in Lake Titicaca. The reeds are first cut and dried in the sun, then sorted and strapped into bundles to form the boat's base and sides. Finally, the sections are bound together with braided reed rope. Sails of reed or cloth are sometimes used to help guide the small craft.

fall is heavy—up to hundreds of inches every year—and pastures and croplands are frequently flooded.

Lakes

Lying partly in Bolivia and partly in Peru, Lake Titicaca is the second largest lake in South America, covering an area of 3,200 square miles. At 12,500 feet above sea level, it is the highest lake in the world navigated by steamboats. The lake is 122 miles long and 45 miles wide. Its shoreline is indented with many bays and coves, and its blue waters are unusually clear. The lake contains 36 islands, of which the

Copacabana is nestled in a hill along the edge of Lake Titicaca. Steeped in Indian lore and traditions, Copacabana sponsors ceremonies and fiestas throughout the year. Legend says that the sun was born in Lake Titicaca and there decided to create the human race.

Courtesy of Inter-American Development Bank

largest are the Islands of the Sun and the Moon.

The Indians travel about Lake Titicaca on boats they make from reeds that grow along the shore. These boats—which look like canoes and are called *balsas*—last only five months, but the Indians use them daily for fishing. Usually only two people ride in a balsa, though it can hold up to four. On short trips, small sails of reed power the balsas. On longer trips, cloth sails are used.

One hundred eighty miles to the southeast and 500 feet lower lies Lake Poopó. Fed principally by the outflow of water from Lake Titicaca through the Desaguadero River, Lake Poopó has one large island. The lake is shallower than Lake Titicaca. Lake Poopó's shores are sparsely populated. South of the lake is the Salar de Uyuni—a vast salt marsh that covers an area of over 7,500 square miles and is several times larger than Lake Poopó.

Flora and Fauna

The llama, alpaca, guanaco, and vicuña—all relatives of the camel—are among the animals native to Bolivia. The first two species were domesticated by the Indians long before the discovery of the New World. The animals are highly prized for their thick fleece, which is used in making the finest overcoats and sweaters. The wild guanaco is hunted for its skin, which, when dressed, makes an attractive rug or robe. The vicuña is sheared for its silky wool.

Bolivia's tropical forests are home to many species of monkeys. Pumas, jaguars, wildcats, coatis (related to the raccoon), tapirs (related to the rhinoceros), sloths, and anteaters roam the country's lowlands. The spectacled bear, named for the yellow facial markings on its shaggy black coat, lives among the wooded foothills of the Bolivian Andes. Many alligators, lizards, and turtles lurk in the warm, tropical lowlands along with numerous snakes—including poisonous pit vipers and giant boa constrictors.

Majestic condors and large eagles soar in the lofty reaches of Bolivia's mountains, while rheas, or South American ostriches, and a species of large stork live in the tropical plains and valleys. Many species of hummingbirds are found in the mountains, and the lowland forests abound with brightly colored parrots and toucans.

Because of its wide variety of climates, Bolivia's vegetation ranges from scanty,

Photo by Organization of American States

Both the alpaca *(right)* and the vicuña *(left)* are native to the South American Andes. The alpaca is closely related to the llama and vicuña and is thought to descend from the wild guanaco. Whereas llamas are used primarily as beasts of burden, alpacas are kept mostly for their wool. Left to graze almost wild on the high plateaus, alpacas have hair that grows from 8 to 24 inches long and can yield up to seven pounds of wool at shearing time each year. Vicuñas are also closely related to llamas but are much smaller and more slender. Vicuñas generally roam in small herds of 5 to 15 females headed by a male and can run up to 30 miles per hour at an altitude of 15,000 feet. Although vicuñas have never been successfully domesticated, they are hunted for their hides and for their wool, which is woven into a very fine cloth.

The tapir, the largest South American land mammal, looks like a pig but has a short, movable trunk, a low, narrow mane, and dark brown skin. Males may grow up to eight feet long. Requiring a constant water supply, tapirs create trails to water sources that are adapted to the contours of the land. They are agile animals who like to swim and dive and are good runners and climbers. Since tapirs feed off of leaves, fruits, and vegetables, they are not aggressive animals and would rather hide in water or dense forest when in danger.

arctic-type trees and flowers to lush, green forests in the tropical lowlands. The country grows many kinds of fruits and vegetables, including varieties raised on both temperate- and tropical-zone farms. The warm lowlands of Bolivia supply commercially valuable trees. These include the rubber tree, from which the raw material for tires is gathered, and the cinchona, whose bark is the source of quinine, an important medicine used to treat fever and malaria.

Capital Cities

LA PAZ

La Paz (population 1 million) is the largest city and the chief commercial center of Bolivia. It also serves as the country's administrative capital, housing most government agencies and the Presidential Palace. One of the most unusual cities in the world, La Paz is situated at the bottom of a canyon at an elevation of 12,001 feet. In the thin air the people of La Paz can clearly see the snowcapped Andean peaks in the distance. The air is so thin that La Paz does not even have a fire department because there is not enough oxygen in the air to spread flames.

The population of the city is about evenly divided between Aymara Indians and those descended from the Spanish, or cholos as Bolivians call the people of mixed Spanish-and-Indian bloodlines. The Aymara, comprising the poorest segment of society, generally live in iron-roofed adobe huts located on less-desirable tracts of steep land in the upper reaches of the canyon. Many of them speak only a native dialect and frequently know just enough Spanish to transact the simplest trade in the marketplace.

Indeed, it is only at the marketplace, one of the liveliest places in the city, that the Aymara interact with the city's more affluent population. At a huge indoor market, the Indians operate stalls selling vegetables, fruits, meats, and flowers. The Indian women who usually operate the stalls knit or weave to pass the long hours,

sometimes accompanied by their children. The marketplace is filled with contrasts. For example, llamas from the highlands bear loads of produce and ice, while mules from the lowlands are heavily laden with oranges and other tropical fruits.

The center of city life is the Plaza Murillo, La Paz's main square, which boasts formal gardens that are faced by the Presidential Palace, the legislative building, and a magnificent cathedral. The cathedral

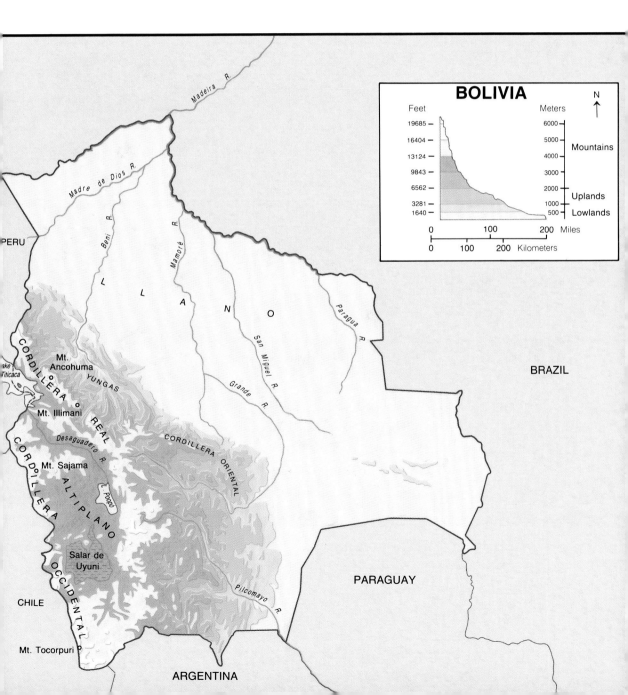

Built in the colonial period, the church of San Francisco in La Paz is richly decorated with ornamentation that suggests both native and religious influences.

Many Indians in La Paz live in colonial-era buildings on narrow, cobblestone streets. These dwellings were originally built as fine homes for wealthy Spaniards.

Located at the bottom of a canyon in western Bolivia's altiplano, La Paz is situated at an elevation of 12,001 feet with a view of snowcapped Andean peaks. It is the highest national capital in the world.

is made of marble and is adorned inside with treasures of religious art. The church of San Francisco, a seventeenth-century architectural masterpiece, also faces Plaza Murillo.

La Paz is a mixture of historic colonial neighborhoods and modern residential areas where well-to-do government officials, professionals, and businesspeople live. The University of San Andrés, located in the heart of the city, has a large outdoor arena that presents concerts and plays every Sunday except in winter.

SUCRE

As the judicial capital of the nation, Sucre—founded in 1538—houses Bolivia's supreme court. Sucre lies high in the mountains at an elevation of 9,000 feet and about 260 miles southeast of La Paz. Originally Sucre was named Charcas, then later Chuquisaca and La Plata, before it was renamed in 1826 to honor General Antonio José de Sucre. Victor of the 1824 battle at Ayacucho, Peru, Sucre helped to end Spanish rule in South America.

Sucre is rich in colonial architecture, including the ornate palace where Bolivia's Declaration of Independence was signed. The city takes pride in the University of San Francisco Javier, founded in 1624, which is one of the oldest institutions of higher learning in the Americas.

Sucre maintains much of its colonial appearance. The city has only 96,000 people and a moderate climate all year long. Its economy depends on the local government-operated oil refinery and cement plant, as well as on farms and factories, which grow and process fruits and cereal grains.

Secondary Cities

In recent years Santa Cruz (population 628,000) has grown to be Bolivia's second largest city—mainly because of the opening up of new farmlands and the creation of new industries. Situated in the middle of fertile, tropical farmlands, the city is hot and humid during much of the year. The temperature can drop abruptly in the winter, however, when cool, dust-laden winds blow north across eastern Bolivia.

Most of Santa Cruz's residents are of Spanish or other European descent—immigrants who have worked hard to develop the area's agricultural potential. Santa Cruz has experienced an economic boom over the last decade, because of the profits from the illegal drug trade, which have been reinvested to create legitimate enterprises. With assistance from the United

Founded in 1538 by Spanish settlers, Sucre is one of the oldest cities of the Americas. The city retains much of its original colonial appearance, with buildings whitewashed today as they were in centuries past. Renamed several times, the city now honors General Antonio José de Sucre (1795–1830), Bolivia's first president after the nation achieved its independence.

21

Courtesy of Inter-American Development Bank

Red-tiled roofs add to the Spanish colonial flavor of Sucre.

central and eastern mountain ranges. Cochabamba is typically Spanish in layout. Its central plaza is surrounded by buildings with arcades and is dominated by a cathedral. The cultural life of the city revolves around the University of San Simón. The city also has several military schools that attract young men who desire prestigious careers as officers in Bolivia's armed services.

About 50 miles southwest of Sucre at an elevation of 13,400 feet—even higher than La Paz—is the old city of Potosí. It was here in 1545 that an Indian named Huallpa discovered the richest silver mine in the New World. As news of the discovery spread, people flocked to Potosí to exploit its riches, hastily constructing a settlement without any order or plan. During the colonial period, huge fortunes in silver were mined at Potosí, and at its peak the city had a population of 160,000. With the silver long ago exhausted, Potosí today (population 114,000) has turned to mining tin and other minerals found nearby.

Another city established after the discovery of silver in 1595 was Oruro, just north of Lake Poopó. Today Oruro (population 196,000) mines tin and copper. Nearby are thermal springs whose waters are said to help treat various ailments.

States, Santa Cruz and the much smaller city of Trinidad (population 28,000) to the northwest—another hub of the drug trade —are attempting to stamp out the production and processing of such dangerous narcotics as cocaine.

Lying midway between Santa Cruz and La Paz, Cochabamba (population 381,000) occupies a fertile plateau between Bolivia's

The residents of Sucre enjoy El Parque, one of the city's many fine parks. A hospital is located in the building with the clock tower. The supreme court building, where the nation's judicial proceedings take place, is situated behind the hospital.

Courtesy of Inter-American Development Bank

Among the ruins of Tiahuanaco is a large, pillarlike statue of the Sun God decorated in low relief. It presides over several similar structures, some reaching more than 20 feet in height. The ruins are believed to have been primarily a ceremonial center rather than an inhabited city. Recently, archaeologists have discovered a network of drainage and irrigation canals that the Tiahuanaco civilization constructed. Scientists are hoping that modern residents can apply the same agricultural methods used by their ancestors to improve crop yields.

Courtesy of Tom Trow

2) History and Government

By studying the skeletal remains of humans and animals, scientists have concluded that people lived in the area of present-day Bolivia at least 10,000 years ago. The early history of those long-ago people is shrouded in mystery. Later, the Tiahuanacans—the first identifiable residents of the area—built a civilization on the south shore of Lake Titicaca.

Archaeologists believe that by roughly 500 B.C. a flourishing settlement had been established at Tiahuanaco, where huge stone ruins attest to the presence of a people with substantial engineering skills. The most impressive ruin is an enormous gateway, known as the Gate of the Sun. Nearby is a large carving of the Sun God, bearing a double staff and presiding over

23

The most impressive monument at the Tiahuanacan ruins is the Gate of the Sun. Carved out of a single block of stone weighing nearly 10 tons, the enormous structure is ornamented with an unusual, low-relief frieze featuring the Sun God over the doorway. The meaning of the intricate symbols surrounding the Sun God is unknown.

Skilled as stonecutters and sculptors, the ancient Tiahuanacans moved decorated stones into place without the aid of wheels. In contrast, these men working under the supervision of archaeologists struggle with a 35-ton slab.

an army of 48 lesser figures. In the immediate area there are other structures made of stones weighing more than 100 tons that were cut and ground to a smooth finish. The structures may have been temples—evidence of a civilization with centralized political and religious control.

The Inca Empire

According to tradition, Manco Capac and his sister-wife, Mama Ocllo, founded the Inca Empire in the thirteenth century and became the originators of a family dynasty that lasted for nearly 500 years. The Incas ruled from Cuzco in southern Peru through a progressive system that balanced the needs of the central government with those of local authorities. Each year, for example, officials of the central government estimated the amount of land needed to raise food and gave a sufficient parcel of land to each family. The balance of land was reserved for the state. The Incan

Carved faces protrude from the wall of this partially underground temple. Tiahuanacan masonry reveals some of the most skillful workmanship in South America and employs the earliest use of metal to link stones together. Between square sections of stone blocks stand upright monoliths (single blocks of stone), which may originally have formed part of a continuous wall.

Photo by Don Irish

peasants were required to cultivate this land before working on their own.

Although they lacked modern tools, the Incas were master builders, and the ruins of an elaborate system of roads, irrigation tunnels, and terraced mountain slopes still exist. The construction of such public works required a knowledge of advanced mathematics. Learned engineers must have presided over projects built by unskilled workers.

During the fifteenth century, the Incas embarked on a campaign of military expansion. Within a hundred years, they were

Independent Picture Service

It took 30,000 Indians 80 years to complete this Incan fortress begun in 1438. They quarried the stone, cut it into interlocking shapes—like a jigsaw puzzle—and put it in place without using mortar to hold the pieces together. Characteristic of Incan architecture, the window on the left is in the shape of a trapezoidal niche—the opening is almost a square, but the base is wider than the top so that the top can easily be closed off with a single long slab.

Independent Picture Service

The Incas used every drop of water from the mountain streams—for drinking purposes, for the Lord Inca's bath (*shown here*), and for the irrigation of their agricultural terraces. The water was led downward, stage by stage, using stone half-pipes, as seen in the spout above.

masters of an empire that stretched 2,000 miles along the west coast of South America and probably included 4.5 million people. By the year 1500 they had conquered an uncounted number of tribes of differing languages and customs and had united them into one of the world's great empires. The highlands of present-day Bolivia comprised the Incan province of Kollasuyo. In the lowlands to the east of the Andes, however, there were scattered tribes that were never conquered by the Incas.

The Colonial Era

The conquest of the Incas began in 1527 when Francisco Pizarro and Diego de Almagro set sail from Panama in search of the fabled riches of the Andes. Upon finding gold used as ornamentation every-

where, Pizarro returned to Spain to organize the conquest of the Incas. At the time the Inca Empire was still recovering from a bloody civil war. The dispute had begun when two brothers, Atahuallpa and Huáscar, disagreed over which of them would succeed their father, the Lord Inca, to the throne.

By the time the Spaniards returned with 120 foot soldiers and 80 horsemen, Atahuallpa had killed Huáscar. The Spaniards arranged to meet with the victorious brother, but instead they ambushed him and took him captive in 1532. Despite the Incan payment of a huge treasure in gold and silver to ransom their leader, the conquistador Pizarro had Atahuallpa executed. The Spaniards then assumed control of the leaderless Inca Empire, which included the territory of present-day Bolivia.

Early during Spanish rule, silver was discovered in enormous quantities near Potosí, an event that had far-reaching consequences for the native groups. The Spaniards forced large numbers of Indians to work in mines under brutal conditions. During the period of peak production from 1572 to 1630, the output of the mines at Potosí often exceeded seven million silver pesos annually and accounted for approximately 70 percent of the mineral exports of the Viceroyalty of Peru—which included Bolivia during Spanish rule. Potosí became famous for its fabulous riches.

In the meantime other settlements were established in Bolivia. A system of large haciendas (plantations) was developed, with Indians forced to work the land as slaves. Many Indians died either of mistreatment or of diseases introduced by the Spaniards. For the most part the Indians quietly endured their miserable lot in life under Spanish colonial rule, though they harbored deep anger and hatred against their exploiters.

In the late 1700s a series of insurrections broke out when the Indians of the Andes, led by Tupac Amarú (José Gabriel Condorcanqui)—a descendant of the last Lord

At a village near Tiahuanaco, the town walls and buildings are still constructed out of adobe.

A colonial-era church faces the main plaza, which is enclosed by a brick wall, in a village near Tiahuanaco.

During early Spanish colonial rule, wealthy families had haciendas, or large estates. Near the main house, trees and graceful archways surrounded the residence. Indians were forced to work the land on these huge plantations.

Inca—tried to drive out the Europeans and reestablish the Inca Empire. Some 40,000 Indians besieged La Paz for more than 100 days in 1781, but finally they were brutally suppressed. Never again did the Indians try to regain their former territory.

The War of Independence

The Indians were not alone in desiring independence from Spain. On May 25, 1809, the people of the capital city of Chuquisaca (the modern city of Sucre) revolted and established their own government. This set in motion similar uprisings in La Paz, Cochabamba, Oruro, Potosí, and Santa Cruz.

For almost 15 years there was intermittent warfare between the Spaniards born in Spain and those of Spanish descent born in the New World, called Creoles. During the course of the fighting Spanish authority gradually weakened. But the fate of Bolivia and Peru was decided by an outsider, Venezuelan-born general Simon Bolívar. After his victories in Venezuela, Colombia, and Ecuador, Bolívar entered Peru and won another victory on the plains of Junín on August 6, 1824. Four months later Bolívar's lieutenant, General Antonio José de Sucre, won the Battle of

Independent Picture Service

The entrance to the colonial-era church at Copacabana on Lake Titicaca reflects the influence of the Moors — Arabs and North Africans who ruled Spain for 500 years and who affected much of Spanish architecture.

president of Bolivia, Andrés Santa Cruz, the son of a minor Spanish official and María Calahumana, who claimed to be a direct descendant of the last Inca. Santa Cruz, who served as president from 1829 to 1839, brought peace and order to Bolivia. His administration oversaw the creation of universities at La Paz and Cochabamba as well as colleges devoted to medicine and science. New penal, civil, mining, and commercial codes were established. Santa Cruz reorganized the nation's finances, encouraged trade and manufacturing, ordered the nation's first census, and had Bolivia's first general map drawn. He launched an impressive road-building program, which included the construction of bridges over difficult mountain passes.

Santa Cruz's ultimate ambition was to become the head of a confederation combining both Peru and Bolivia. But the governments of Argentina and Chile supported the Peruvians in opposing Santa

Ayacucho in Peru, which marked the end of Spanish rule in Bolivia and Peru.

The Republic

On August 6, 1825, what had formerly been Alto (Upper) Peru became an independent republic, named Bolivia in honor of the great liberator. General Bolívar himself drafted a constitution for the new nation that was ratified by its first congress in 1826.

Bolívar ruled Bolivia for six months, showing great genius as an administrator, before transferring his authority to Sucre. The following year Sucre was chosen as the country's first president under the new constitution. He served in office for two and a half years before resigning to take part in independence struggles elsewhere.

After a series of short-lived presidencies, Sucre was followed by the first native-born

Courtesy of Organization of American States

Antonio José de Sucre was Bolivia's first constitutional president.

29

Born in Venezuela on July 24, 1783, Simon Bolívar is called "the Liberator" for his role in freeing South American countries from Spanish rule. After gaining independence in 1824 for Peru—which at that time included Bolivia—Bolívar organized southern Peru into a new republic, which was renamed Bolivia in his honor.

Courtesy of Inter-American Development Bank

Cruz, and all three countries combined forces to defeat the Bolivian troops at the Battle of Yungay in 1839. Thus ended Santa Cruz's dreams of confederation. The Chileans imprisoned him and later exiled him to France where he died.

Territorial Losses

The defeat at Yungay marked the beginning of 40 years of strife and insurrection in Bolivia, where bitter feuds arose between military officers, landowners, and mineowners. In trying to achieve exclusive power, these groups actually paralyzed the national economy and deepened internal divisions between Indians, whites, and cholos (those of mixed Indian-and-Spanish bloodlines), while doing nothing to further Bolivia's national identity.

To fill Bolivia's lack of a strong leader, unprincipled military officers tried to build a sense of national purpose by taking on external foes, which diverted popular atten-

tion from problems at home. This course proved disastrous for Bolivia, leading to the loss of more than half of the nation's territory. During the War of the Pacific (1879–1883) between Peru, Chile, and Bolivia, Bolivia lost to Chile the nitrate-rich lands along the Pacific coast and its territorial access to the Pacific through its own ports. Bolivia has never resigned itself to this loss.

While Bolivia was trying to recover from its loss of Pacific coastline, Brazilians were settling Bolivia's jungle state of Acre along the Brazilian-Bolivian border. Responding to the demand for rubber that occurred around the turn of the century, Brazilians conspired with local Bolivians in Acre to declare the independence of this rubber-rich state from Bolivia. These Bolivians announced their desire to be annexed to their powerful neighbor, Brazil. In 1903, by the terms of the Treaty of Petropolis, Brazil acquired a large chunk of Bolivia with hardly a struggle.

Wiser from this loss but still lacking strong leadership, Bolivia again plunged into turmoil on the local political scene. The country's fortunes improved only during World War I, when the demand for Bolivian tin and beef increased tremendously. Bolivia sold its minerals and meat exclusively to the Allies, formally breaking off diplomatic relations with Germany in 1917, when a ship carrying a Bolivian minister was torpedoed by a German submarine.

The Chaco War

The economy of Bolivia continued to boom following World War I because of the discovery and development of oil resources in southern Bolivia by foreign-owned companies. But, as in earlier Bolivian history, the profits of good times were shared by only a relatively small proportion of the people—mainly Creoles (those of pure European ancestry) and cholos who had reached middle-class status. The Indian majority

Photo by Don Irish

In the colonial section of La Paz, intricate balconies carved out of wood are still suspended from some of the buildings.

Photo by Don Irish

The Museo Costumbrista in La Paz features miniature displays that depict incidents in the history of the surrounding area.

31

remained outside of the economic mainstream, denied access by their lack of education and by their inability to speak Spanish, the language of commerce.

There was little political stability in Bolivia. One leader would form a new party and lead a revolt and government takeover, only to be overthrown in turn by someone else within a year or two. Amid this chaos, military officers invited a German military mission to organize and train the Bolivian army.

Meanwhile, increasingly bloody border clashes were developing with the forces of neighboring Paraguay to the southwest. The cause of the skirmishes was the rumored oil wealth in the Gran Chaco region. Thus, the origins of the Chaco War lay in conflicting claims to ownership of a region that had little proven natural wealth and whose boundaries had never been mutually agreed upon by Bolivia and Paraguay.

With substantial oil reserves suspected —but not proven to this day—ownership of the Chaco, the haunt of Indians who identified with no nation, assumed great importance. When war broke out in 1932, Bolivians were confident that their much larger army, led by the German general Hans Kundt, would prevail. The war proved to be bloody. It lasted for three years, and by the time the last shot was fired, some 50,000 Bolivians were dead— 15,000 more casualties than Paraguay had lost.

As a result of a 1938 treaty with Paraguay, Bolivia lost nearly a quarter of its remaining national territory. The defeat deeply wounded the Bolivian psyche. The war, however, also brought about important changes in the military, political, and cultural life of Bolivia. For the first time in Bolivian history, European descendants, Indians, and cholos were brought together fighting for the same cause. Indians became aware of their own political role. In the wake of the war, Bolivia had 10 presidents in 16 years and experienced the for-

Independent Picture Service

Named after the day in 1809 when the independence movement began, Sixteenth of July Avenue is the most important thoroughfare in La Paz.

When Bolivia became independent, it claimed much more territory than it has today. A succession of wars with the surrounding countries led to the loss of its Chaco region to Paraguay and its Amazonian lowlands to Brazil. The most serious loss was that of Atacama—now in Chile—with its seaport of Antofagasta and its rich nitrate deposits.

mation of left-wing political parties and unions seeking social justice. In time this increased concern for justice would lead to demands for revolutionary change.

The Revolution of 1952

Of the many political organizations that sprang up after the Chaco War, the National Revolutionary movement (MNR) became the most powerful. After a brief but bloody revolt in April 1952, the MNR seized power and immediately introduced sweeping revolutionary changes. The army, which had meddled in Bolivian politics all too frequently, was reduced. Under President Victor Paz Estenssoro, all Bolivians were eligible to vote for the first time in Bolivian history.

SOCIAL REFORM

The Bolivian government assumed control over the tin mines, which had for many years strongly influenced the country's political and economic life. The Indians of the nation were granted full civil rights. A broad program of land reform granted peasants title to their own tracts of land. Education and social welfare programs began to provide schools and health care for all Bolivians.

The greater stability of the Bolivian government encouraged the United States to provide substantial financial assistance to Bolivia. With foreign aid Paz Estenssoro and his successor from the MNR, Hernán Siles Zuazo, introduced sizable public works programs. Railways were built to neighboring Brazil and Argentina. A new highway linked Santa Cruz—along with its potentially productive farmlands—to Cochabamba and the commercial centers of the highlands to the west. With government assistance, settlers from other land-poor areas of the nation converted huge tracts of jungle into farmlands.

For 12 years, from 1952 to 1964, Bolivia appeared to be on the road toward progress, fashioning a political system that would enjoy a wide base of popular support. But unfortunately, deepening divisions occurred within the leadership of the

Reforms enacted after the revolution of 1952 brought education to more children in rural areas.

MNR. In November 1964, a military junta overthrew President Paz Estenssoro, just as he was beginning his third presidential term. Paz Estenssoro's vice president, General René Barrientos Ortuño, participated in the coup and emerged as the leader in the subsequent junta.

Barrientos, a charismatic leader, seemed able to provide the strong hand the times demanded. During Barrientos's administration, Ernesto (Che) Guevara, the Argentine-born guerrilla who had played a leading role in the Cuban revolution, attempted to stir up insurrection in Bolivia. With the aid of U.S. military advisors, the Bolivian army put down the guerrilla movement. Che Guevara himself was wounded and captured on October 8, 1967, and shot to death two days later.

Barrientos's success in defeating the guerrilla movement made him popular with the U.S. government, which was determined to prevent the spread of Cuban-style Communism to other Western Hemisphere nations. Barrientos was also viewed as a savior by Bolivia's landowners and aristoc-racy—all those who wanted to maintain the existing distribution of wealth.

Recent Events

After Barriento's death in 1969, Bolivia experienced a series of takeovers by left- and right-wing factions. In 1980, General Luis García Meza seized power. García Meza suspended congress, prohibited all activity by political parties, and stifled the labor unions.

After being implicated in drug trafficking, García Meza was overthrown. To reestablish order, Bolivians turned to the aging leaders of the 1952 revolution, re-electing Hernan Siles Zuazo in 1982 and Victor Paz Estenssoro in 1985.

At the same time, Bolivia's economy was collapsing, with the annual inflation rate reaching 24,000 percent. Paz Estenssoro managed to bring this ruinous inflation under control. Under his successor, Jaime Paz Zamora, the government passed laws intended to spur foreign investment. In 1990 the government announced plans to sell state-run companies to private owners. This was intended to help the Bolivian treasury and increase employment.

Bolivian workers, however, resisted privatization of large state companies, particularly in the mining industry. As a result, the privatization plan has stagnated. Nervous about Bolivia's political instability and difficult labor relations, foreign investors turned away from Bolivia. In the early 1990s, Paz Zamora's administration also suffered a series of corruption scandals. Although the economy has improved, Bolivians still suffer uncertainty about the future of their country.

Government

In accordance with its 1967 constitution, Bolivia has executive, legislative, and judicial branches of government. Executive power is vested in a president who is elected to a four-year term and who is as-

Argentine guerrilla Che Guevara was executed in Bolivia.

sisted by a cabinet. The president and vice president are elected by direct popular vote. Since 1952 all Bolivians over age 21 have been eligible to vote. The president is required by law to make a tour of the country at least once during his term in office to study the needs of the people.

Legislative authority is in the hands of a bicameral (two-house) congress, which consists of a senate and a chamber of deputies. Congress meets once a year for a 90-day session. The country is divided into nine departments, or states, and the senate has three members from each department, or 27 in all. They are elected by the people and serve for six years. One-third of the members are elected every two years.

Each of the nine departments of Bolivia is governed by a prefect, who is appointed by the president to a four-year term. The departments are subdivided into provinces, each one under the authority of a subprefect, who is also appointed by the president. The provinces, in turn, are divided into cantons, each governed by a corregidor, who is chosen by the prefect. Each city has a mayor, appointed by the president, and a city council elected by the people. The government of the entire country is thus kept firmly in the hands of the national president, who appoints the prefects, the subprefects, and the mayors.

Although Sucre is the judicial capital of Bolivia, the seat of government is in La Paz, where all legislative and executive functions are carried on. Only the supreme court meets in Sucre. The judicial branch of government also has departmental and lower courts.

The Legislative Palace in La Paz houses the senate and the chamber of deputies.

Photo by José Armando Araneda

At festivals women dress in bright clothes and men wear their best suits.

3) The People

The total population of Bolivia is about 7.8 million, of which more than half is pure Indian. The country is underpopulated, and the population distribution is very uneven. The high plateau of the Andes, with its fertile valleys and sloping hillsides, is much more densely populated than the rest of the country. Statistically, less than one person per square mile lives in the hot eastern lowlands.

With an urban population of 51 percent, Bolivia has a lower percentage of people living in cities than do many Latin American countries. Roughly 41 percent of the entire population is under 15 years of age. (In the United States only 22 percent are under 15.) The large percentage of young people in Bolivia is due to two factors—the high birth rate and a life expectancy of only 61 years. The high death rate among infants, however, has slowed population growth. Bolivia's rate of infant mortality—89 per 1,000 births—is the highest in Latin America. Most homes in the country

36

have no heat and no sanitary facilities. For these reasons, many babies die before they are a year old.

European Descendants

Bolivia's topography has discouraged Europeans—many of whom are unaccustomed to high altitudes—from immigrating to the country in the twentieth century. During the 1930s, however, a few thousand Germans, Spaniards, and Poles escaped Nazi Germany to settle in the cities of La Paz and Cochabamba. Many of these immigrants later went on to Peru or Argentina. Most of Bolivia's European population are descendants of Spaniards who came during the colonial period. Only about 15 percent are of pure European ancestry, while cholos comprise 30 percent of the population.

The Indians

The Indians of Bolivia come from three different ethnic groups—the Quechua, the Aymara, and the Guarani. Each group speaks a different language, and only educated Indians speak Spanish at all. Originally the Aymara—who now comprise 17 percent of the population—formed part of a group of people who lived north of Cuzco, Peru. After becoming part of the Inca Empire, they settled near Lake Titicaca. Though

These boys wear chullos, or knitted caps with earflaps, which help to keep them warm in the Bolivian Highlands.

Photo by José Armando Araneda

37

the Aymara and the Quechua (who make up 25 percent of the population) have lived in the highlands of Bolivia for centuries, they have never intermixed. The Guarani, who are fewer in number, live in the lowland regions of the east.

Indian Clothing

Despite the inroads of civilization, many Indians maintain their traditional clothes and customs. The women wear their hair in long pigtails, with a soft derby hat on their heads. They wear an apron over a bright skirt with many underskirts, which help to keep the women warm and which stand out like hoop skirts. Their garments are of many bright colors and often include something red. They frequently wrap a beautiful, fringed, Spanish shawl around their shoulders, and they almost always

In the warm climate of the Amazonian lowlands, clothing is generally made of lightweight cotton rather than the heavy wools worn in the cooler highlands.

This Indian man wears a warm sheepskin vest. Animal hides are often worn as outer garments in the highlands, where evenings are cool throughout the year, and both days and nights are bitterly cold in winter.

Throughout the Bolivian altiplano women wear derby hats, full skirts with many layers, and either traditional fringed shawls or a blanket for warmth. This woman is probably carrying a baby in the pack on her back.

In rural areas of Bolivia, many homes —such as this one made of stones and adobe mixed with straw—follow a design used for centuries.

carry a pack or a baby on their backs. Indian good-luck dolls made of clay are tucked in with the bundles on their backs. Even in winter many of the Indian women go barefoot.

While the women keep warm with many petticoats and woolen shawls, the men wear a woolen poncho, often a red one. The Indian men usually wear shoes as well as a chullo, or knitted cap with earflaps. The Indians have unusually large chests, which is nature's way of allowing them to adapt to living in a high altitude. The Indians are usually beardless and broad faced, and many of them look Asian. The men often ride a mule, but the women always walk.

Daily Life

Bolivia's Indians and cholos continue to live off the land. Even with agrarian reform and the distribution of parcels of land, many Indians are unable to raise enough food for their families on poor soil and steeply inclined tracts. About two-thirds of all Bolivians live in poverty. In the early 1990s the average yearly earnings per person stood at about $600, making

Bolivia's small wealthy class enjoys comforts familiar to other Western, industrialized countries such as the United States. Here, a family of Spanish descent living in Santa Cruz entertains friends.

Bolivia one of the poorest South American countries. The Bolivian government is attempting to improve the life of Indian farmers by providing information about more advanced technologies for tilling the land and about improved seed and fertilizers to boost production.

The Indians do their laundry in roadside streams, spreading garments out on the ground to dry in the bright sun. Indian women carry their babies on their backs —along with supplies and needlework—no matter what they do or where they go. Indians who have small farms live in adobe houses with roofs of thatched straw. Those who work in the mines live with their families nearby in huts made of stone and mud.

Most of Bolivia's aristocracy live in the cities. Although they make up a small percentage of the country's population, the wealthy control the government and most substantial business enterprises. The well-to-do often send their children abroad for higher education. The life of the urban middle class, which includes some cholos as well as European descendants, is in sharp contrast to the lives of the Indians. Those who are financially secure live in much more spacious and comfortable housing, and often they employ domestic servants.

Food

In the fertile land around Lake Titicaca, two crops—quinoa and oca—provide the basic food of the Indians. These plants have been raised in Bolivia for centuries. Quinoa, a strong, weedlike plant with a heavy head of large seeds, grows four to five feet high. After being roasted and

Courtesy of David Mangurian

In this street in La Paz, modernity clashes with tradition, as Bolivia's predominantly Indian population undergoes a change of dress and ways. The city's Indians live in their own cultural section, which intersects the area for whites and mestizos only at places like the cobblestone street market, where Indians buy and sell goods.

Many Indians eat soup, potatoes, and ocas almost every evening. Soups are often made with wheat flour or noodles. Most Bolivian dishes are hot and spicy.

Photo by José Armando Araneda

Photo by José Armando Araneda

Cooking facilities for many of Bolivia's Indians are makeshift. These women cook outside, feeding their tiny stove with reeds for fuel.

On the Island of the Sun in Lake Titicaca, these Indians gather the chuño, or dried, shredded potatoes, which they have been preparing for several days.

boiled, quinoa seeds make a delicious porridge that has a nutlike taste different from other cereal grains. Oca—a slender, fleshy root from two to four inches long—resembles a small, pink sausage and is a relative of the wood sorrel.

The Indians of Bolivia have worked out their own way of freeze-drying potatoes and ocas for later use. They spread the vegetables on the ground to freeze at night and to thaw in the sunlight. For several days, the Indians trample the vegetables with their bare feet to squeeze out the moisture. Finally only the light, dry husk is left. It keeps for a long time. Travelers carry ocas when they go on a long journey, for they can be cooked quickly. The Indians call the preserved potatoes chuño and use them in stews and soups. Potatoes are a staple among people who live in the

A farmer sells his produce—chuño and oca—in a market in La Paz.

Outdoor shopping is extremely popular, because it provides opportunities for social gatherings as well as a marketplace for all needed articles. Here, also, those who seek herbal cures can find the traveling doctor.

Andes, since this vegetable flourishes in altitudes above 14,000 feet.

While Bolivia's Indians eke out a meager diet of chuño, ocas, and quinoa, the nation's aristocracy, in contrast, feasts on meat and fresh fruits and vegetables. A meal for the well-to-do might begin with a hearty chicken soup seasoned with Indian herbs. This might be followed by a plate heaped with several slices of roasted hindquarter of kid (young goat), along with vegetables covered with a pungent cream sauce. Dessert usually consists of baked plantain (a type of starchy banana) and freshly picked papaya (a large, oblong, yellow fruit) or some other fruit from the tropical valleys.

Health

The Bolivian government has a small budget for health care. The number of hospitals, clinics, medical posts, and doctors is low compared to the size of the population. In the early 1990s, there was one physician for every 1,775 people.

Because few trained physicians visit the highland region, a group of so-called traveling doctors employs folk cures and medicines found in the Bolivian Highlands. These doctors are said to have influence over the supernatural, and patients insist that the doctors have performed miraculous cures.

Among the illiterate population, traveling doctors are highly respected. They travel amazing distances in groups of 8 or 10, carrying their medicines in woven bags slung over their shoulders.

At markets and fairs, these doctors sell bundles of leaves, roots, seeds, resins, and charms made of bone, wood, stone, and metal. Many of the preparations are made up of several plants mixed with fats, powdered bird feathers, hair, and other ingredients. In addition to medicines, the traveling doctor has charms to solve almost any personal difficulty. Some charms are made of roughly carved stone, and each one is in the form of a hand grasping some object. For example, a hand grasping corn will ensure a good corn crop, and a hand grasping money will guarantee financial success.

Religion and Fiestas

Most Bolivians are Roman Catholic and attend church services. The people also continue to follow ancient Indian religious beliefs. The mixture of these religions fosters many superstitions.

Bolivia has many fiestas throughout the year. Scarcely a week passes when villagers cannot attend one in their own village or a nearby town. Although fiestas are supervised partly by the Catholic Church and are held to venerate a particular saint, the activities may be as much Indian as Christian.

Fiesta dances are largely of Spanish origin, with local elements added. In the highlands, the cueca, or handkerchief dance, is the most popular. In this dance, the partners circle round and round each other, linking their arms at intervals—much as in

Photo by José Armando Araneda

Men often provide music for dancing at festivals. These boys, with their mandolin, guitar, and accordion are ready to play for any occasion.

Wearing the traditional, red woolen poncho and a brightly colored chullo, this Indian man from Lake Titicaca entertains his friends by playing a zampoña, or vertical flute made of reed pipes.

Photo by José Armando Araneda

a North American square dance—while waving a handkerchief in tiny spirals above their heads. The cueca is danced at all major fiestas and lasts from midmorning until early evening.

All through the year Bolivians look forward to the excitement of Carnival, the biggest fiesta held just before Lent, a period of fasting and repentance leading up to Easter. During Carnival, music and dancing go on for several days. Men wear their best black suits, while women are colorfully dressed in vivid full skirts and shawls with bright embroidery.

Independent Picture Service

Independent Picture Service

Pre-Columbian and Christian traditions merge in many parts of Bolivia. Here, a mining official *(left)* models the traditional Oruro devil's mask, worn by the Oruro Devil Fraternity. The fraternity is organized to honor the Virgin of Socavón, patroness of Bolivian miners. In the background is a replica of a mine entrance. Folk dancers at Huarisata *(right)* wear traditional masks of a slightly less grotesque style.

A family wedding is also an occasion for great merrymaking in Bolivia. After the church service, the couple leads the procession to the home of the bride, where a banquet has been prepared at the expense of the bridegroom and his parents. A band provides music for dancing, which continues all day and far into the night.

Literature

Bolivia's colonial Spanish literature was largely made up of chronicles and religious works written by priests and administrators. The leading Bolivian writer after independence in the nineteenth century was Gabriel René-Moreno, who wrote histories, biographies, essays, and vivid descriptions of Bolivia's towns and countryside. Although René-Moreno was a harsh judge of Bolivian politics and was prejudiced against the native Indians, he is honored by Bolivians today for his contribution to historical documentation.

In the early twentieth century Ricardo Jaime Freyre and Franz Tamayo dominated Bolivian literature. Whereas earlier writers had focused on the misery of the Indians, Tamayo emphasized their nobility. Bolivian writing became more preoccupied with these native themes as the twentieth century progressed.

A feature of Bolivian festivals is the piñata, a huge paper container full of toys and trifles, which, when punctured, showers its treasures on the merrymakers.

After the Chaco War, which had awakened in Bolivians a need for greater unity and nationalism, writing became more political. Some authors criticized the government. Others, such as Augusto Céspedes and Fernando Ramírez Velarde, dealt with the social issues of the impoverished Indian and cholo populations. Since the 1952 revolution social protest writings have either glorified the revolution and its victory or criticized the government for making too few or too many changes.

Education

Primary education is free and compulsory for children ages 6 to 14 in Bolivia, but the public schools do not meet the nation's needs. About 83 percent of primary-age students attend school, while only 27 percent of secondary-age students continue their studies. Since most young Indian children cannot speak Spanish, they must learn Spanish as a new language.

Nevertheless, the number of adults who can read and write is steadily increasing.

Futbol (soccer) is a popular sport among Bolivian schoolchildren.

In 1990 about 22 percent of the people remained illiterate, with illiteracy much higher in rural areas than in cities. About 880,000 pupils attend primary school, and 227,000 attend secondary school. In addition there are 97,000 students enrolled in higher education. Eight state and two private universities exist in Bolivia.

Classrooms are often informal in the Amazonian lowlands, with teachers and pupils alike attending class barefoot. This class meets in a village on the Madre de Dios River, which flows for a thousand miles before emptying into the Amazon.

Many of Bolivia's commercial transactions take place in the nation's open marketplaces.

4) The Economy

Though Bolivia has a wealth of natural resources still to be developed, several factors have held back the country's economic development. The nation lacks its own seaport, which would ease the flow of trade. Difficulties of transportation and communication caused by the mountainous terrain also inhibit economic development. But the most important obstacle to progress has been the failure to achieve political stability. If the government can maintain a program of steady economic reform, all Bolivians may begin to benefit.

At present, farming employs nearly half of Bolivia's workers. Many agricultural workers, however, must wrest a living from poor soil. Another 34 percent of the employed work for the government or in service industries, including health care and education. Nineteen percent of the work force is engaged in industry and commerce, including the processing of foods and minerals and the fabrication of textiles and other products.

The 4 percent who work in the mines and in the petroleum and natural gas fields are the country's most productive workers. These activities account for two-thirds of the nation's legal exports. To control the income from these resources, Bolivia has established two governmental agencies. One agency oversees the production of the nation's oil and natural gas fields, the other oversees the production of mines, which provide valuable export products and which have figured importantly in the

Mining for tin at San José mine in Oruro requires considerable work above – as well as below – ground. This device – called a jig – separates the tin concentrate from its waste material. The ore is heavier and settles to the bottom of the jig, and the waste is shoveled off the top.

At Catavi mine, one of the largest mines in Bolivia, workers clear a drainage ditch from the side of the mine's railway tracks.

country's economy since the discovery of the New World.

Mining

It is said that almost every known mineral may be found somewhere in Bolivia. Currently silver, gold, tin, tungsten, lead, mercury, nickel, antimony, zinc, copper, bismuth, uranium, and iron are taken from the ground, while nonmetallic substances such as asbestos, limestone, mica, salt, and sulfur are also successfully exploited.

Most of Bolivia's mining operations take place in the narrow belt of land 500 miles long and 60 miles wide that runs from north to south along the Cordillera Real. The only metal found in large amounts outside this belt is iron, which is found at Mutún on the border of Brazil. Tin is Bolivia's principal mineral asset, and the country is the only large-scale source of this metal in the Western Hemisphere.

49

After the ore is separated from the waste, the ore is loaded into cars to be processed. This mine is located near Potosí. Before the Spaniards arrived, Indians dug out rich veins of silver, but now only zinc is found here. The Bolivian government has recently added a processing plant to the mine that concentrates the zinc to a purity of 55 percent. Miners remain the only organized segment of Bolivian labor. Through their trade unions they exert tremendous political influence.

Before 1952 the three largest tin mines were under the control of three families called the "tin barons." They built immense fortunes and controlled much of the country's economic and political life. Foreign engineers were brought in to direct the work, and Indians were hired to do the actual mining. After long agitation and negotiation, the mines were taken over by the government in 1952.

The tin-producing countries of Southeast Asia and of Africa obtain most of their ore from shallow mines near international waterways. Bolivia's tin, on the other hand, is mined from veins deep underground at altitudes of from 12,000 to 17,000 feet above sea level. The mines are separated from points of shipment on the coast by rugged mountain ranges. A further handicap is the fact that Bolivia's purest metal ores have already been mined, and the metal content of the remaining ores is decreasing at a rate of 4 percent each year. All of these factors have contributed to the deterioration of Bolivia's earnings from tin.

A British engineer observes a family mining enterprise, where a sluice box – a trough with a grooved bottom into which sediments settle – is used to recover tin concentrate from the flowing water.

This plant in Cochabamba, in central Bolivia, manufactures cement pipes for water and sewage, which will help to improve the often-poor sanitation systems of Bolivian cities and towns.

By the late 1980s, Bolivia's income from tin had decreased by 25 percent, and the mines were operating at only half of their total capacity. Although tin at one time provided Bolivia's largest export income,

Workers drill an oil well at Santa Rosa, about 50 miles from Santa Cruz.

it now ranks third among legal exports after petroleum products and natural gas. The government has been trying to promote the mining of other metals to relieve the economic dependence upon tin. Minerals still make up nearly half of the country's legal exports, although mines employ less than 5 percent of the work force.

In the 1990s, the government began closing inefficient state-run mines and laying off mine workers. Bolivia has passed new laws to encourage foreign investment by international mining companies. Nevertheless, the mine closings are causing serious hardship to miners.

Oil and Natural Gas

The first indication that petroleum lay beneath Bolivian soil appeared in 1895, but no oil concessions were granted until 1916. Not until 1925 was the actual existence of oil deposits confirmed on land grants held by the Standard Oil Company. Production, refining, and export of oil were put in the hands of a Bolivian firm in December 1936. The next year, the rights that had been given to the Standard Oil Company in 1921 were withdrawn and became the property of the government. In

51

In a refinery in Santa Cruz, an operator makes notes of the gauge readings.

A vertical view shows the inside of a drilling rig, where a team of workers are changing a drill bit.

1969 the concessions previously operated by the Bolivian Gulf Oil Company were nationalized. All oil production is now in the hands of the government. The principal oil fields are in the departments of Santa Cruz, Chuquisaca, and Tarija.

Total production of oil exceeds eight million barrels annually, part of which is exported to Argentina. A refinery in Cochabamba, which gets its crude oil from Camiri, has a capacity of 8,000 barrels daily. Bolivia thus produces sufficient gasoline, kerosene, and lubricants for its own use and is exporting an increasing share of its production. There are small refineries in Sucre, Santa Cruz, Camiri, and Bermejo. In Cochabamba a factory now produces containers for gasoline and petroleum-based lubricants.

Natural gas is Bolivia's most important export, and by the early 1990s gas represented 35 percent of the country's export earnings. A natural gas pipeline connects Santa Cruz to the Pacific coast at Arica, Chile, and natural gas also flows by pipeline to Argentina. A gas pipeline to Brazil has also been constructed.

Agriculture

Bolivia's farmland, like its mines, was once held almost entirely by a few rich families. The injustices, poverty, and hunger resulting from this system helped to spark the revolution in 1952. The following year, a land reform act similar to earlier land reforms in Mexico and Guatemala went into effect. As a result, the peasants acquired acreages of their own, but they did not change their old-fashioned methods of farming. Even though they now own small tracts of land, the peasant farmers are bound by tradition and handicapped by illiteracy. Land in Bolivia is in great demand, but often the farming units are too small to operate economically. The government is seeking to help the farmers through vocational education, technical assistance, and transportation improvements.

Independent Picture Service

The bicycle is a symbol of progress in the altiplano. These young campesinos (rural dwellers) have cycled from their farm homes to attend a meeting of community leaders conducted by a United Nations expert *(second from right)*.

Bolivia is a leading producer of coca leaves, which are used to make the drug cocaine. Indians chew the leaves to deaden sensations of hunger and cold and to increase their energy. Coca exports range from 46,000 to 69,000 tons annually. Smugglers transport most of the raw coca leaves to neighboring Latin American countries, where they are processed in makeshift laboratories. Most refined cocaine is exported to the United States. To discourage coca-growing, the United States has offered grants to farmers who switch to other crops. This policy has met resistance from many Bolivian farmers.

The agriculture of the valleys has wide variations, depending on the altitude and location. La Paz is easily accessible from the northeastern valleys, which have better soil than the valleys of the highlands.

An Indian woman wields her hoe with one hand, as she clutches her child with the other.

Independent Picture Service

Coca plants are widely grown in Bolivia, where the Indians chew on the leaves for energy. In recent years much of the yearly coca crop has been processed into the dangerous drug cocaine and shipped illegally to the United States.

A woman carries a machete—an essential tool of life in the tropics. Farmers use these long, vicious-looking knives to clear and plant their family's plot of cultivated land. Machetes are also used to cut poles and thatch for homes and firewood for cooking. Where there are no butchers, these knives serve to carve meat, and women trim the husks off coconuts with machetes to obtain nourishing milk to feed their babies. In her other hand the woman carries another precious possession—an enamel teapot.

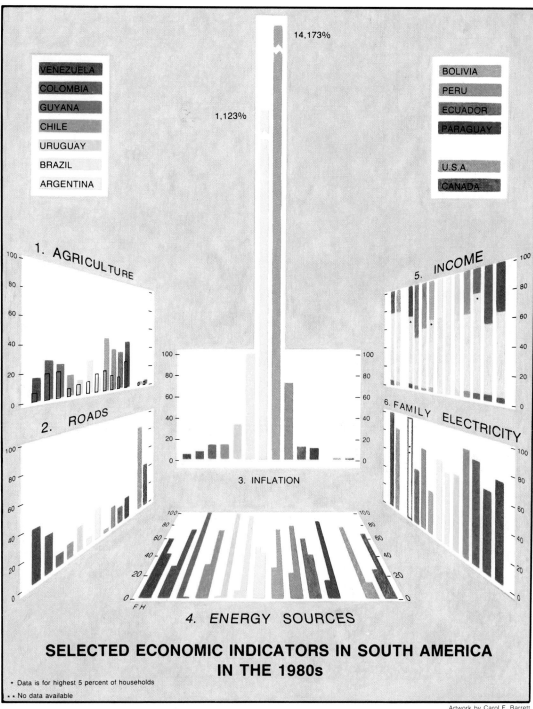

14,173%

1,123%

VENEZUELA
COLOMBIA
GUYANA
CHILE
URUGUAY
BRAZIL
ARGENTINA

BOLIVIA
PERU
ECUADOR
PARAGUAY

U.S.A.
CANADA

1. AGRICULTURE

2. ROADS

3. INFLATION

4. ENERGY SOURCES

5. INCOME

6. FAMILY ELECTRICITY

SELECTED ECONOMIC INDICATORS IN SOUTH AMERICA
IN THE 1980s

* Data is for highest 5 percent of households
** No data available

Artwork by Carol F. Barrett

This multigraph depicts six important South American economic factors. The same factors for the United States and Canada are included for comparison. Data is from *1986 Britannica Book of the Year, Encyclopedia of the Third World, Europa Yearbook,* and *Countries of the World and their Leaders, 1987.*

In GRAPH 1—labeled Agriculture—the colored bars show the percentage of a country's total labor force that works in agriculture. The overlaid black boxes show the percentage of a country's gross domestic product that comes from agriculture. In most cases—except Argentina —the number of agricultural workers far exceeds the amount of income produced by the farming industry.

GRAPH 2 depicts the percentage of paved roads, while GRAPH 3 illustrates the inflation rate. The inflation figures for Colombia, Guyana, and Brazil are estimated. GRAPH 4 depicts two aspects of energy usage. The left half of a country's bar is the percentage of energy from fossil fuel (oil or coal); the right half shows the percentage of energy from hydropower. In GRAPH 5, which depicts distribution of wealth, each country's bar represents 100 percent of its total income. The top section is the portion of income received by the richest 10 percent of the population. The bottom section is the portion received by the poorest 20 percent. GRAPH 6 represents the percentage of homes that have electricity.

Many Indian farmers still work the land using old-fashioned methods. Here, two oxen pull a crude plough that makes a single furrow, while the woman walks behind, planting seeds.

Besides the staple foods that the peasants eat, such commercial crops as cacao, coca, and coffee are produced in the valleys, as well as tropical fruits and cassava (a plant with a fleshy, edible root). The area around Santa Cruz now produces enough rice and sugarcane for its own needs, with a small surplus for export. Sugarcane was introduced to Bolivia at an early date, and much of it traditionally has been used for making rum.

In the basins and valleys near Cochabamba, fairly good soil enables the farmers to grow wheat, corn, and barley, as well as vegetables and tropical fruits, which are sold to the cities in the highlands. Valleys to the south are less-densely populated and grow few crops for market. Near such large cities as Sucre and Tarija, however, cereals and fruits are grown. Cattle and goats are also raised and furnish meat and milk for market.

Livestock

The domesticated llama and alpaca have been used by the highland Indians since prehistoric times. These animals are sim-

A livestock specialist shows shepherds how to use a dredging gun to rid sheep of intestinal parasites.

ilar to the camel in their endurance and usefulness in transportation. Their wool is used for making clothing, especially for fine coats, and for making rope. Their meat is dried and preserved but seldom eaten fresh.

Cattle are raised in many parts of Bolivia. In the highlands and the high valleys, oxen are used to pull wagons. When no longer useful, these animals are killed and used for food. In a few areas of the lowlands cattle are bred for beef on a large scale. In 1983 there were 4.2 million head of cattle, mostly in the departments of Santa Cruz and El Beni. Attempts have been made to encourage a dairy industry in the Cochabamba region.

Sheep are raised mostly in the highlands, where they graze freely on natural pastures year round. The chinchilla, a native rodent prized for its luxurious fur, is also raised, and its skin is exported. Other livestock raised on a smaller scale include horses, mules, donkeys, pigs, rabbits, goats, guinea pigs (for food), chickens, turkeys, and ducks.

Forestry

Although Bolivia has some of the best timber resources in the world, the forests are exploited only minimally since many of them are beyond the reach of modern transportation. The best forests are found on the eastern slopes of the Andes and along the rivers of the Amazon Basin. In these forests large areas of tropical trees —both evergreens and hardwoods—grow.

Rubber trees yielding a high quality of rubber grow wild in the forests of Pando and El Beni in northern Bolivia. Brazil nuts grow wild on trees that often reach

The Amazonian forests are rich in hardwood trees, but the timber industry remains to be fully developed. As more Indians from the altiplano resettle in the lowlands, however, more forestry resources can be exploited.

This man is a representative from a government-sponsored agency that promotes productivity in rural areas and supplies Indians with loans. This woman is signing a loan to buy fertilizer—a somewhat unusual sight in Bolivia's male-dominated society.

Courtesy of Inter-American Development Bank

100 feet tall. In parts of southeastern Bolivia there are forests of abundant hardwoods, such as walnut and mahogany.

The eucalyptus was introduced from its native Australia in the nineteenth century, and today occasional eucalyptus groves are found near the cities in the highlands. Some eucalyptus trees are grown near Cochabamba and Sucre for fuel and for supports in mines.

Manufacturing

In the 1960s Bolivia increased its production of cotton and cotton products. At the same time the government also took a more friendly attitude toward private enterprise, which led to the development of many small manufacturing businesses. Cement factories, food-processing plants, shoe factories, and various other new industries were introduced, some of them powered by hydroelectric energy developed in the departments of La Paz and Cochabamba.

In 1967 Bolivia joined the Latin American Free Trade Association and the regional Andean Group to help improve its economic position. Bolivians continue, however, to rely heavily on imports of

Built with financial and technical help from the Inter-American Development Bank, the hydroelectric plant at Coraní, near Cochabamba, supplies electricity to a large area of west central Bolivia and has improved the industrial manufacturing capability of the region.

Courtesy of Inter-American Development Bank

manufactured items, many of which are brought in illegally. It is unknown how many Bolivians make a living by smuggling in processed consumer goods, but they may number in the thousands. The chief imports are lard, flour, cooking oil, mining machinery, pharmaceuticals, paper products, textiles, and iron and steel products. Because Bolivia has no seaports, its imports and exports pass through the ports of Arica and Antofagasta in Chile, Mollendo and Matarani in Peru, La Quiaca on the Bolivian-Argentine border, and through ports on rivers flowing into the Amazon.

Transportation

Bolivia, like other Andean countries, has changed its form of transport during the twentieth century from oxcart to aircraft. The nation is served efficiently by several international airlines that land at El Alto Airport, the highest commercial airport in the world. Only five miles from the city of La Paz, El Alto is 12,000 feet above sea level.

The Bolivian national airline, Lloyd Aéreo Boliviano, connects cities throughout the highlands and plains and also has

Courtesy of Museum of Modern Art of Latin America

Sheep raising for wool and meat is a major economic activity in the Bolivian Highlands. This shepherdess rewinds wool that has been recently dyed by running it out on a homemade spindle. By repeatedly throwing the wool to the ground, she unsnags the threads. The smoothed strands are wound onto a skein, which eventually will be woven into cloth.

Courtesy of Inter-American Development Bank

Lydia Choquehuanca uses fine alpaca wool yarn—which she has spun herself—to weave a rug. The Indians of Bolivia are renowned for their beautiful woven textiles.

59

Most Bolivians either walk or rely on public transportation to get around. In the rugged mountains of Bolivia, trucks often transport people *(left)*. Truck drivers without a load routinely stop to offer people walking along the highway a lift. A railroad *(below)* now links the major cities of the altiplano. This train has stopped at a point near Cochabamba, where some of the passengers have come out to stretch.

flights to nearby countries. Air transportation is of vital importance to Bolivia because of its inland location, high elevations, and the scarcity of good roads and rail facilities.

The Pan-American Highway, which links North and South America, crosses Bolivia from the south to the northwest. A new highway, completed in 1990, also links Bolivia with the Chilean port of Arica, an important transfer point for Bolivian exports.

Foreign Aid

Great prosperity came with World War II and its demand for two important Bolivian products—tin and wolframite, from which the metal tungsten is extracted. Rising

Two-wheeled carts drawn by oxen are still a common sight in parts of Bolivia—in Trinidad, for example, a city in the Amazonian lowlands.

Mules are the most reliable means of transport available in many areas of the Bolivian Highlands where roads have yet to be built.

prices and strikes led to the growth of the leftist National Revolutionary movement. When the Bolivian economy collapsed in 1953, a dreadful inflation followed. This was caused by the government's costly social-welfare scheme and by continual wage increases. Fearing that Bolivia would turn toward Communism and against Western democracies, the United States started giving financial aid in 1953. In 1956, in collaboration with the United States and the International Monetary Fund, Bolivia instituted a stabilization plan.

To help Bolivia realize the goals of its 1952 revolution and to forestall an anti-Western, Communist takeover, the United States provided substantial support to Bolivia during the 1960s under the Alliance for Progress. Such international financial agencies as the World Bank and the Inter-American Development Bank continued financial support during the 1970s, despite the emergence of political turmoil on the Bolivian scene. Bolivia's develop-

61

ment ambitions were further fueled by loans from privately owned foreign banks, many of them in the United States.

Up until the early 1980s the Bolivian government hoped to repay the loans through the profits from the nation's expanded mining and energy sectors. But unfortunately the global recession of the early 1980s lowered world prices for minerals and energy exports, and Bolivia found itself paying interest on its foreign debts in 1982 equal to about 53 percent of all its earnings from exports. As a result, by 1984 the nation was confronted with extremely high inflation. By the end of 1984 Bolivians were paying nearly 13 times the prices they had paid on the same consumer products at the beginning of that year.

Illegal Drug Trade

The spiraling growth of illegal drug trafficking further complicated the troubled economy. By the mid-1980s this illicit com-

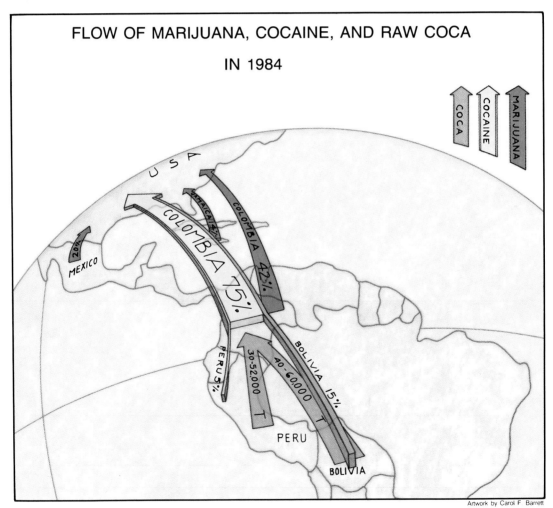

This chart shows the country of origin and the percentage of total U.S. supplies of marijuana and cocaine that are sent to the United States from Latin America. Although coca is cultivated in Colombia itself, the chart also illustrates the movement of tonnages of Bolivian and Peruvian coca to Colombia for processing into cocaine. (Data from *Narcotics Intelligence Estimate 1984* compiled by the U.S. Drug Enforcement Administration, Washington, D.C.)

At this isolated laboratory in Bolivia, dried coca leaves are made into a paste from which cocaine is extracted for shipment to the United States.

merce was estimated to bring Bolivia three times the profit of its leading mineral export. Moreover, the profitable drug trade generated corruption. Despite lack of control over its most important source of revenue, the Bolivian government was faced with the impossible task of imposing financial stability.

Amid economic anarchy, with inflation running over 14,000 percent annually, Bolivians turned to one of the leaders of the 1952 revolution, Victor Paz Estenssoro. At 78 years of age, Paz Estenssoro was elected in mid-1985 to a fourth term as Bolivia's president. As chief executive he moved quickly and deliberately to turn the nation around.

Economic Turnaround

Under Paz Estenssoro's administration, Bolivia invited in U.S. troops to help root out the trade in illicit drugs in 1986—at a time when, according to Paz Estenssoro, the industry was earning Bolivia $600 million annually, compared to $500 million from legal exports. In another bold move, Paz Estenssoro laid off 7,000 miners out of a total mining work force of 20,000 during his first year in office. The president clearly and directly explained the rationale for the cutbacks. He said that Bolivia could not go on indefinitely producing tin for $10 a pound when it was selling on the world market for only $2.48 a pound.

Paz Estenssoro's economic policies—including the laying off of thousands of government employees and the reforming of the country's tax system—brought inflation down. At the same time, the president created a high rate of unemployment. In the early 1990s, President Jaime Paz Zamora faced the challenge of maintaining control of inflation and finding work for jobless people. He also pressured Bolivians to stop growing coca and producing cocaine. By 1990 Bolivia's annual earnings from the drug trade had been cut in half.

The United States has offered millions of dollars to Bolivia's coca-leaf growers, if they will plant a different crop. The funds would help make up for some of the money the farmers would lose by changing to a less profitable crop. Until Bolivia can replace income earned from coca-leaf production and from its declining mining operations, the nation's economy will continue to suffer.

Index

Acre, 30
Agriculture, 8, 10–11, 13, 18, 21, 24–26, 33, 39–40, 48, 52–53, 56–57. *See also* Coffee; Fruit; Grain; Livestock; Oca; Potatoes; Quinoa
Alliance for Progress, 61
Almagro, Diego de, 26
Alpaca, 10, 16–17, 56–57, 59
Altiplano. *See* Highlands
Alto Peru, 29
Amazon Basin, 13, 33, 38, 47, 57, 61
Amazon River, 13, 47, 59
Andean Group, 58
Andes. *See* Mountains
Architecture, 20–25, 27–29, 31
Argentina, 10, 29, 33–34, 37, 52, 59–60
Aristocracy, 8, 28, 34, 40, 43, 50, 52
Armed conflicts and wars, 9–10, 28–34, 47, 52, 60–61, 63. *See also* Ayacucho, Battle of; Chaco War; Guerrilla movement; Revolution of 1952
Art, 20–21, 23–24
Aviation, 59–60
Ayacucho, Battle of, 21, 28–29
Aymara, 11, 18–19, 37–38
Balsas, 15–16
Bolívar, Simon, 8, 28–30
Bolivia
   name of, 29–30
   national identity of, 8, 30, 47
   size and location of, 10, 30, 32,
Brazil, 7, 10, 13, 30, 33, 49, 52
Cathedrals and churches, 19–22, 27, 29
Cattle, 13, 56–57
Chaco, 13–14, 32
Chaco War, 31–33, 47
Charcas. *See* Sucre
Chile, 7, 10–11, 29–30, 33, 52, 59–60
Cholo, 18, 30–32, 37, 39–40, 47
Chuquisaca, 52
Cities and towns, 9, 21–22, 28, 49–52, 56, 58–61
Climate, 4, 7–8, 11, 14–16, 18, 21, 36, 38
Cocaine and coca plants, 9, 11, 13, 22, 53–54, 56, 62–63
Cochabamba (city), 22, 28–29, 33, 37, 51–52, 56–58, 60
Cochabamba (department), 58
Coffee, 11, 56
Colombia, 28, 62
Commerce and trade, 7, 18, 29, 32–33, 40, 48
Communications, 48
Communism, 34, 61
Condorcanqui, José Gabriel. *See* Tupac Amarú
Congress, 29, 34–35
Constitutions, 29, 34
Copacabana, 16, 29
Cuzco, 24, 37
Dance, 44–46
Declaration of Independence, 21–22
Diseases, 8, 26
Drugs, illegal, 9, 11, 13, 21–22, 34, 53–54, 62–63. *See also* Cocaine and coca plants; Marijuana

Economy, 8–9, 13, 21, 31–34, 48–63
Ecuador, 28
Education, 21–22, 32–33, 37, 40, 43, 47, 52
El Beni, 57
Elections, 34–35, 63
Energy and fuels, 9, 21, 31–32, 48, 51–52, 58, 62. *See also* Natural gas; Petroleum and oil
Estenssoro, Victor Paz, 34, 63
Exports, 7, 9, 34, 48, 51–53, 56–57, 59, 62–63
Festivals, 36, 44–46
Fish, 9, 16
Flora and fauna, 16–18
Food, 9, 40–43, 48, 56–57
Foreign aid, 33–34, 61–63
Foreign-owned companies, 31, 51
Forests and forestry, 11, 14, 16, 18, 57–58
Fruit, 19, 43, 56
Gate of the Sun, 23–24
Germany, 31–32, 37
Government
   buildings, 18–19, 22, 35
   corruption, 7, 9, 34, 63
   economic and social reform, 9, 29, 33–34, 48, 50–52, 58, 61
   instability, 30–34, 48, 61–63
   land reform and resettlement programs, 13, 33, 39–40, 52, 58
   structure, 34–35
Grain, 21, 56
Guanaco, 16–17
Guarani, 37–38
Guerrilla movement, 34, 63
Guevara, Ernesto (Che), 34
Health and medicine, 11, 18, 22, 29, 33, 36, 43–44, 48, 51, 59
Highlands, 8, 10–11, 13–14, 17, 19–20, 22, 26, 33, 36–38, 43–44, 53, 56–61
History, 23–34
   colonial era, 7, 20–22, 26–28
   Inca Empire, 7–8, 24–26, 28
   independence, 7–8, 10, 21, 28–30, 32
   pre-Inca, 23–24, 56
   twentieth century, 30–34
Housing, 4, 18, 20–21, 27–28, 39–40, 54
Illiteracy, 43, 47, 52
Imports, 58–59
Incas, 7–9, 11, 24–26, 29, 37
Indians, 4, 7–9, 11, 13, 15–16, 18–20, 22–26, 28–29, 31–33, 36–47, 50, 53–54, 56–59. *See also* Aymara; Guarani; Incas; Quechua; Tiahuanacans
Industry, 21, 29, 48, 51, 57–59
Inflation, 9, 34, 61–63
Inter-American Development Bank, 58, 61
International Monetary Fund, 61
Islands, 15–16, 42
Jungles, 7, 30, 33
Lakes, 9, 15–16, 22–23, 37, 40, 42
Languages, 8, 18–19, 26, 32, 37, 47
La Paz (city), 4–5, 7–8, 12, 18–21, 28–29, 31–32, 35, 37, 40, 42, 53, 59
La Paz (department), 58

Latin American Free Trade Association, 58
Literature, 46–47
Livestock, 10, 16–17, 56–57, 59, 61. *See also* Alpaca; Cattle; Llama; Sheep
Llama, 16–17, 19, 56–57
Lowlands, 8, 11–14, 16, 18–19, 26, 36, 38, 43, 57
Maps and charts, 6, 19, 33, 55, 62
Marijuana, 13, 62
Markets, 7, 19, 40, 42–43, 48, 56
Meza, Luis García, 34
Military service, 22, 32, 34
Minerals and mining, 7–10, 22, 26, 29–31, 33, 34, 40, 46, 48–51, 58–60, 62–63. *See also* Natural gas; Petroleum and oil; Silver and gold; Tin
Mountains, 10, 21, 29, 48, 50, 60
   Ancohuma, 11
   Andes, 7, 11, 13–14, 16–18, 20, 26, 36, 43, 57, 59
   Cordillera Occidental, 11
   Cordillera Oriental, 11, 22
   Cordillera Real, 11, 22, 49
   Illimani, Mount, 5, 11
   Sajama, 11
   Tocorpuri, Mount, 11
Music and drama, 21, 44–46
National Revolutionary movement (MNR), 33–34, 61
Natural gas, 9, 48, 51–52
Oca, 40–43
Oruro (city), 8, 22, 28, 46, 49
Pacific Ocean, 7, 30, 52
Pando, 57
Paraguay, 7, 10, 13–14, 32–33
People, 36–47
   characteristics of, 8–9, 18, 39
   clothing of, 36–40, 45
   economic classes of, 7–8, 19, 28, 31–32, 34, 39–40, 43, 52
   ethnic background of, 8, 18, 28, 30–32, 36–38, 40
   standard of living of, 4, 14, 18–21, 36, 39–41, 47, 54, 61
Peru, 9–10, 15, 21, 24, 26, 28–30, 37, 59–60, 62
Petroleum and oil, 9, 21, 31–32, 48, 51–52
Petropolis, Treaty of, 30
Pizarro, Francisco, 26
Political parties, 32–34
Population, 14, 18, 21–22, 36–38, 40, 47, 56
Ports, foreign, 33, 59
Ports, lack of, 33, 48, 50, 59–60
Potatoes, 41–43
Potosí (city), 22, 26, 28, 50
Presidents, 21, 29–30, 32–35, 63
Quechua, 37–38
Quinoa, 40, 42–43
Railroads, 33, 49–50, 60
Rainfall, 14–15, 60
Recreation and sports, 9, 11, 22, 44, 47
Religion, 44–46
Revolution of 1952, 9, 33–34, 47, 52, 61, 63
Rivers, 13, 16, 47, 57, 59
Roads, 12, 25, 29, 33, 60–61
Roman Catholic Church, 44
Rubber, 18, 30, 57

Salar de Uyuni, 16
Santa Cruz (city), 21–22, 28, 33, 39, 51–52, 56
Santa Cruz (department), 52, 57
Sheep, 10, 56–57, 59
Silver and gold, 8, 22, 26, 49–50
Slavery, 8, 26, 28
Spain, 7–8, 16, 21, 26, 28–30, 37, 50
   influence of, 18, 20–22, 27, 31, 37–39, 44, 46
Sucre, 21–22, 28, 35, 52, 56, 58
Sucre, Antonio José de, 21, 28–29
Sun God, 23–24
Supreme Court, 21–22, 35
Tarija (department), 52
Territorial losses, 7, 10, 30–33
Textiles, 48, 59
Tiahuanacans, 23–25
Tiahuanaco, 9, 23–25, 27
Tin, 8, 31, 33, 49–51, 60, 63
Titicaca, Lake, 4, 9, 15–16, 23, 37, 40, 42
Topography, 10–14
Trade unions, 34, 50, 63
Transportation, 48–50, 52–53, 57, 59–61
Tupac Amarú, 26
United States, 9, 22, 33–34, 36, 39, 54, 61–63
Universities, 21–22, 29, 47
Venezuela, 8, 28, 30
Vicuña, 16–17
Wool, 10, 16–17, 38–39, 57, 59
World Bank, 61
Writers, 46–47
Yungas, 11–12, 14
Zamora, Jaime Paz, 34
Zuazo, Hernán Siles, 34